ONE DESIRE

ONE DESIRE

A Book of Collects

ERIC BROTHERIDGE

Sydney & Carver

Introduction

collect ('kä-likt, also 'kä-lekt) - a short prayer

I began writing the collects collected in this book in March of 2020. Initially I wrote them as an exercise in sermon-preparation. I tried to interpret, focus and condense the scripture reading and my sermon-thoughts for the upcoming Sunday into the collect form. The thinking was as follows: if i could get my point across in five short phrases, then my sermon of one hundred and fifty to two hundred lines had a better chance of being understood.

My first, formal exposure to the collect form came in seminary; reading Janet Morley's *All Desires Known* for a class on Christian worship. I wrote my first collect, a Collect of Mourning, as an assigned exercise:

> God of Creation,
> You are the valley through which we walk.
> Embrace us with your presence of peace
> in this time of death,
> that our feet may carry
> on the steps of life's journey
> through Jesus Christ, the healer of all hurts.
> Amen.

The collect form is an ancient form for prayer - indeed for human communication - and has been around since the time when human beings first said prayers for ancestors, for crops and for success on the hunt, and for the daily chores and activities of life. In its simplest form a collect has five parts:

> The address
> The acknowledgement
> The desire
> The motivation
> The closing

The parts of a collect answer the questions for a basic human request. Who is being spoken to? What power does that person have to answer the request? What is the request or what does the speaker want? Why is the speaker requesting what they want? And, a closing of some simple form.

Here is a favorite collect of mine from childhood:

> Mom,
> best baker in the world,
> let me have a cookie
> because I am hungry,
> please.

The five-part form of the collect is designed to express one desire; from the simple language of a request for a warm cookie, right out of the oven, to the formal theological expressions found in the collects of Thomas Cranmer in *The Book of Common Prayer*.

Whereas I began writing collects as a sermon-writing technique, as 2020 unfolded, the collect form became a way for me to maintain my sanity and focus in a tumult-filled time. First, COVID-19. Then the reactions following the death of George Floyd. The economic crisis. The Presidential election season. Masks or no masks. Freedom from or freedom for. Wildfires in Australia and California. Not one but three hurricanes at the same time. The Beirut explosion. Governmental intransigence. Deaths of beloved leaders, friends and mentors.

There were days where my prayer list (let alone the prayers of the members of the congregation I served during this 2020 time) could run on for pages. As my morning ritual began to include writing a daily collect, it was a "relief" to pick...just one thing; to express one desire and one desire only. Just one thing to ask of God, the creator, to anybody or anything that would listen. Just one request. Focusing on "just one desire" became very freeing for me spiritually and allowed me to get through difficult days.

The collects collected here play off a line of scripture, either from the larger scripture reading used for a Sunday worship service or from some of my own personal favorite scriptural passages. My hope is that in reading these collects, these poems, you will also find some freedom, some peace, some hope and a renewed sense that one desire is enough.

The Collects

On either side of the river is the tree of life...
- Revelation 22:2

Maker of
pines and pin oaks,
burning bushes and the Joshua tree,
evergreens and the piñon,
who centers every tree
in our Garden of Creations;
gather roots around us,
intertwine each with the other,
so fruit of all flavors
drops like jewels
through grasping fingers
into open hands.
Amen.

...and Jesus said to her, "Give me a drink."
- John 4:7

God,
who thirsts
and meets us
in our driest places,
may my words, deeds and thoughts
be wellsprings that overflow,
because the parched
cry out to be well.
Amen.

And they drove him out.
- John 9:34

God who meets us
when the world doesn't need us
rub mud on our eyes
so we see with your eyes.
Amen.

"Unbind him, and let him go."
- John 11:44

God the Weaver
of Creation's
very fabric,
who knots and unknots,
guide us by the thread of life
to the heart's desire of the other
so we can unwrap
the woes of this world
allowing Beauty
to escape.
Amen.

...and when he had looked around at everything...
- Mark 11:11

God,
whose glance covers the cosmos
with attention,
give us a gaze that aspires to leave nothing out
of the order and chaos that surrounds us
for the sucking void hides what can be precious.
Amen.

Suddenly Jesus met them and said, "Greetings!"
- Matthew 28:9

God of the Garden Tomb,
Mover of earth and stone and air,
Speaker of "Hello",
in the morning and
in our mourning
you step out and greet us
as if we were neighbors
stepping out to get our mail
after a long day of work.
Make "Hello" natural again
because we don't know each other.
Amen.

"...will do greater works than these..."
- John 14:12

Doing God,
living, dying and living again God,
do you "do" us?
Like, if we don't "do" it
then your will "does" not get "done"?
If so, "do" us
because so many
don't "do" anything.
Amen.

...a sound filled the entire house...
- Acts 2:2

Creator of the Universe,
filling an entire house
with the whoosh of yourself.
Is there a rush of wind
in your absence?
A withdrawal that
sucks the life out of us?
Leaving us empty
and staring
at the empty rooms
where we thought
there had been something
just a moment before.
Whoosh me
for I need wooshing.
Amen.

Now when they heard this, they were cut to the heart...
- Acts 2:37

O, Divine butcher
splitting our breastbones
wide open to get to
the guts of our heart,
give us ears to hear
the clean cut
of the sharp edge of truth
for fat of ugly lies
lies heavy on us.
Amen.

Not a needy person among them.
- Acts 4:34

God who wanted to know God,
crying out into the Void,
"I AM!"
needing company,
how can you need
and we, your creation, not need?
Our daily bread is just that,
daily bread.
A dollar can only be stretched so far
before being ripped apart.
The need of the brutes
makes so many even more needy.
Dare we ask for more, God?
God, can you give more?
For need, our need,
is part of the fabric of
your way.
Amen.

"A good tree cannot bear bad fruit, nor can a bad tree bear good fruit. Every tree that does not bear good fruit is cut down and thrown into the fire."
- Matthew 7:18-19

Creator of all trees,
who declared after the forest was complete,
"It is good!"
whence bad fruit?
Yes, we will die
from eating the fruit of the tree of knowledge
but we need all the knowledge we can get on this day
and we need to "Get into the forest again"
as Lawrence wrote
because we are dropping like gorged flies
from the bad fruit scattered and strewn
wantonly and recklessly upon the ground.
Amen.

"The young men came and wrapped up his body, then carried him out and buried him.
- Acts 5:6

God of all ages,
God of the child who
Jesus takes into his arms
declaring,
"Whoever welcomes one such child
in my name welcomes me,"
why, then, do Jesus' followers
watch, teach and ask that child
to become a young human that
wraps up dead bodies,
carries dead bodies,
and buries dead bodies,
bodies created by the church?
I am done watching bodies
wrapped up, carried out and buried in the ground,
out of sight,
out of mind.
Too many young children
have grown up to be dead bodies.
Too many young children
have grown up to kill alive bodies.
God, the Bodies of Christs
need more than just "Enough!"
to be carried into Life!
Amen.

"...you shall count off seven weeks; they shall be complete."
- Leviticus 23:15

God who counts the dust,
grains of sand and hairs on our heads,
the stars and our descendants,
your desire for perfect perfection,
seven times seven,
heartens and emboldens.
If
week after
week after
week after
week after
week after
week after
week
may be made complete in your eyes,
then
as this week moves towards its sabbath
count this week
as one week
complete.
Amen.

Now a new king arose over Egypt, who did not know
Joseph. He said to his people, "Look, the Israelite people are
more numerous and more powerful than we."
- Exodus 1:8-9

God, clother of Adam & Eve,
God, gifter of the rainbow,
God, appointer of Abraham,
God, chooser of Joseph,
God, creator of kings,
how can a newly created king not know of Joseph?
Why do idiocy and stupidity seem to always take
the thrones of condemnation and carelessness?
Do you, God, get some perverse pleasure
out of the rare instances where
powerlessness prevails over power?
Sure, the names of the powerlessness
ring across the history of humanity
but the names of those wiped away
with the wave of a hand by those in power
are more numerous
than grains of sand on Crescent Beach
and more numerous
than the countless stars in the universe
and, horrifically, forgotten.
God of upside down power
and God of upended numbers,
the multitudes cry out, Save us!
Amen.

Then we who are alive, who are left, will be caught up in
the clouds together with them to meet the Lord in the air;
and so we will be with the Lord forever.
\- 1 Thessalonians 4:17

God who comes and
Toots His Own Holy Horn,
where angels call
and the faces of earth's multitude turn Heavenward
with the crossed-fingered, hope of rising first,
and those desirous,
with the ticket of their small faith,
of taking a trip on a cloud like a Disney ride,
to the Lord's Forever-Ever-Land,
...Bah! And boo, boo, boo!
You know the Plan.
No one goes until everybody goes.
The notion of The Elect, Your Holy Elect,
kills the least of these
over and over and over
again and again and again.
Speak plainly.
Mean the words of the mountaintop.
Stay with us.
Amen.

Moses took the blood of calves and goats, with water and scarlet wool and hyssop, and sprinkled both the scroll itself and all the people, saying, "This is the blood of the covenant that God has ordained for you."
- Hebrews 9:19-20

Holy Vampire,
who dies on a wooden stake
only to come back to life,
is there anything else
needing to be covered in blood?
Forty deaths in Atlanta?
Sixty-three in Chicago?
Imagine:
the blood of
one hundred and three
sprinkling the asphalt
over the weekend.
Do you have any new,
less bloody,
covenants
up Your sleeve?
Amen.

If, however, you bite and devour one another, take care
that you are not consumed by one another.
- Galatians 5:15

Creator of all food,
Preparer of all tables,
Head Chef,
Maître d',
Spice of All Life,
who lowers the Tablecloth
of ingredients
and the menu
before our very eyes
and declares, Eat!
Do we taste each other?
Take a nibble?
How does one devour another
and not consume another?
We bite and eat each other
because we are starving
for each other.
Perhaps another
menu is in order?
Amen.

Therefore the law was our disciplinarian until Christ came, so that we might be justified by faith.
- Galatians 3:24

Christ,
Eternal with God,
the beginning Word,
through which the Law
came into being,
begotten, not made,
breaking yourself apart
as an example
to discipline your disciples,
saying, You feed them,
feed us
again.
Jews and Greeks,
male and female and other,
struggle with each other,
against each other,
for each other,
as the Law disciplines
again
with each other against each other.
Amen.

I consider that the sufferings of this present time are not worth comparing with the glory about to be revealed to us.
- Romans 8:18

You,
Who suffered on the cross
- some say for our sakes, for my sake -
and died.
Tell me how the point of a nail
through the wrist
compares
to my demon's daily grind and grinding
of this present time
which followed
the grind in the present time of a moment ago
and, if all Hell doesn't break loose,
will be followed by the grind in the next moment in time?
A comparison with future glory is necessary
to keep considering
the sufferings of this present time.
Amen.

What then are we to say about these things?
- Romans 8:31

God who cried pain
into the universe from the cross
and who,
after breaking yourself apart
at the very beginning of time
pealed to the heavens, "I AM,"
and who,
after finishing the early work of creation
declared, "It is good!"
make the words in our mouths
so we may say
something
about these things
that make heaven on earth
...intricate and awkward and grim.
Amen.

...so that you may discern what is the will of God—what
is good and acceptable and perfect.
- Romans 12:2

Will-full, God,
who gives me the ability to discern your will,
is your will singular or plural?
Who is the "you" You are referring to?
For while I may be clear
on what is good and acceptable and perfect,
the plurality of "you,"
the second person's plural,
them, those people and the Others,
discern a different good and acceptable and perfect.
Amen.

And you shall set the bread of the Presence on the table
before me always.
- Exodus 25:30

Presence,
Giver of all presents,
presented on the table
is the bread of the Presence,
presently
uneaten.
If You are not going to eat it
can I have a bite?
Or, if my request smites you as selfish
might I share it with the hungry?
Amen.

...and the thing was suddenly taken up to heaven.
- Acts 10:16

Divine Deliverer, who brings down
"something like a large sheet"
filled with
"all kinds of four-footed creatures
and reptiles and birds of the air,"
a miraculous menu for all to consider,
voicing from above the earthly table,
"What God has made clean, you must not call profane,"
send more of that sheet,
as we failed, for the fourth time,
to read your writing in the heavens.
For upon its removal, the earthly author
turned
the dream of your holy arrangement
into a disappearing act,
even calling the dream,
"the thing."
Amen.

Examine yourselves...
- 1 Corinthians 11:28

Holy Questioner and Divine Judge,
you allowed yourself to be stretched out
upon the Roman cross.
May this bread and this cup
stretch our minds
beyond
the hurt we wish to inflict, so
the divisions that make us hungry to hurt
and the thirst for our own righteousness to be done
come together at a table
to be transformed by filling love.
Amen.

"...and those who humble themselves will be exalted."
- Luke 14:11

Super Self,
While your help
is...helpful...
the abundance of selfie photos
testifies to our own
self-exaltation.
Call it
Personal Deification.
Autonomous acclaim:
"Look how beautiful I am!"
Which I am, I AM?
Amen.

"Listen! A sower went out to sow."
- Matthew 13:3

So, God,
Ground of All Being,
Creator
of the path,
of rocky earth,
of thorns, barbs and bristles,
and of the good soil.
Scorched, withered and choked
seems to be the produce of today
farmed from the labor of our hands and mouths.
Dare we blame the seed?
Ask for new seed?
Amen.

Someone in the crowd said to him...
- Luke 12:13

All-Knowing, All-Seeing, All-Hearing One,
Who said it?
Always the anonymous one.
Again.
Looking to gain by stirring up trouble.
Too many want their lives their way today
- Has this ever not been the case? -
and to have it their way,
mysterious and unknown,
special only to them.
Take care, you reply,
be on your guard
against all kinds of greed.
Amen.

"What is this that I hear about you? Give me an account-
ing of your management..."
- Luke 16:2

Owner, Holder, Possessor,
You have heard nothing about me.
Really.
I have managed the best I can with what I have.
No thanks to you.
All thanks to you.
We all hear some strange things
about all of them.
And they hear some strange things
about all of us.
Please, account for us and for them
so we may balance.
Amen.

"This fellow welcomes sinners and eats with them."
- Luke 15:2

Divine Maître d'Création,
how hard it is to type "î" and "é" on an English keyboard;
about as hard as dining with "Them".
Did you have to let them in?
Did you have to seat them?
Did you have to serve them?
(Did you cook for them?
Make bread?
Pour wine?)
Look how the place is empty
because
folks/diners/eaters disappeared.
How about you come and eat with them too?
Amen.

...precept upon precept, line upon line, here a little, there
a little.
- Isaiah 28:13

Unutterable Utterer,
Isaiah passes along some strange words;
even stranger coming from you, *baruch ha'shem*,
whom we call The Word.
Worse,
the mad purpose behind this nursery rhyme
is to make us "fall backward, be broken,
and snared and taken."
Heaven protect us!
(But wait, that's where these words come from!)
G*d,
we already have a babble of words.
We need words like:
clarity and coherent,
pure and precise.
A word
simple and spirit-full, like Light
luminescent.
Amen.

"But at midnight there was a shout, 'Look! Here is the bridegroom! Come out to meet him.'"
- Matthew 25:6

Perfect Ten,
You dally, dawdle, delay
- who knows where doing who knows what -
and then,
as in the fairy tales of old,
you appear at midnight
(presumably with both shoes on?)
as if the wedding invitation said,
"Hors d'oeuvres and mingling begin at 12:00 a.m."
It is difficult to come out to meet you at such a late hour
when we are all tucked in, lights out,
sleeping our lives away.
Bring oil, please.
Amen.

"Friend, how did you get in here without a wedding robe?"
- Matthew 22:12

Party-Thrower Extraordinaire,
It sounds like a typical party
- or the usual call of your reign -
most aren't interested,
some don't want to attend,
others have to be dragged,
still more begged,
then enticed:
"Come as you are!"
But upon seeing me,
you cry, Friend!
and end by throwing me
into the outer darkness.
(I thought my purple velvet rags
would be perfect wedding attire.)
Is it any wonder, Host with the Most,
that few want to join in the festivities?
Amen.

"Lord, here is your pound."
- Luke 19:20

Pound-provider, Dollar-deliverer, Gold-giver,
What if we don't want your money?
We have and more is given to us
though we try and try to dispose of it
- mostly for our own selfish needs -
or else store your wealth in six by six by eight units
or make a deposit of a number with zeros that follow.
Ask the average Jane on the street,
"Do you have enough?"
A silly question,
"What if we don't want your money?"
Deliver us.
Amen.

I will utter dark sayings from of old...
- Psalm 78:2

Hearer, O Hearer,
It's the dark sayings from of old,
that frighten us.
Children hide for fear of what the next adult parable
havocs in their tiny lives;
though curiosity draws them out
to see what the crazy ancestors always do next.
Decrees. Laws. Commandments.
A messy mix more fit for eating
than to place into ears that hear.
Continue to work your works, God,
so we will not forget.
Sometimes forgetfulness saves.
Amen.

Some wandered in desert wastes...
- Psalm 107:4

Desert Waterer,
I fish at the side of your river
while ash falls from the sky.
Is this that moment
between pools of water
and parched land
where your hand moves
forced by a decision woven
that time long ago
when you declared, "It is good!?"
Tears move down dry skin on so many faces
weathered, beaten, gathered,
waiting for good things.
Deliver us from distress.
Amen.

...more than enough shame from the proud.
- Psalm 123:4

Bull-ier of bullies,
the proud, the haughty,
the puffed-up, contemptuous ones,
still get all the attention
at the playground monkey bars.
Tomorrow,
on the way out to recess,
trip them up and bloody their noses
so they must go instead
to the nurse's office.
Amen.

God will turn the hearts of parents to their children and
the hearts of children to their parents.
- Malachi 4:5

Heart-Turner,
we could throw ashes upon ourselves wailing.
for the hearts of our children
turn away, go onward and ahead;
yet a child's heart desires
to join with Spring's unfolding flowers.
Make the blooms jewels;
Gifts of the parents.
Amen.

Go, eat your bread with enjoyment, and drink your wine
with a merry heart; for God has long ago approved what you
do.

- Ecclesiastes 9:7

God,
who sets the table before us,
move the heavy-laden from our minds
move the care-laden from our hearts,
create a feast of bread and wine
to share with those we cannot touch.
Amen.

Moses would put the veil on his face again.
- Exodus 34:35

Countless-Faced One,
who speaks to us through Moses,
whose face shining bright with holy knowledge
makes the people afraid,
remove the masks that enshroud our hearts from love;
place them as veils, as masks, over our lips
to protect all others from our cruel words
and thoughtless deeds.
Amen.

God made us. We belong to God.
- Psalm 100:3

God of the Infinite,
"Variety is the spice of life"
yet how often do we replace "we" with "me"?
Make us anew
so that I once more belong with others
and,
with others,
belong to You.
Amen.

Wisdom is better than weapons of war.
- Ecclesiastes 9:18

Word of Wisdom,
inspire insight
ignite intelligence
in the war of wise words
for Folly stands at the podium
again
with the sweat of black death
rolling down his cheek.
Amen.

Whoever observes the wind will not sow; and whoever regards the clouds will not reap.
- Ecclesiastes 11:4

Worker of Wonders and Wonder,
who moves as wind through Chaos
and who fills the skies with cloud-shapes,
we lie awake in torment
guessing with thought,
Will the coming day
be a day for sowing
or a day for reaping?
Make whatever work we choose
be fruitful
and may we have fruit
as the wind whispers
and the clouds roll.
Amen.

All words are wearisome; more than one can express.
- Ecclesiastes 1:8

Word,
words weary today
and yesterday I awoke just fine.
While the world whirls in babble
give me one sentence
with subject and predicate
with a direct object
and especially an indirect object
that receives those kind words.
Amen.

Is there a thing of which it is said, "See this is new?"
- Ecclesiastes 1:10

Maker of all things new,
does finishing the work of creation on the seventh day
mean nothing thereafter is new?
Or, does the Teacher mean:
though the spectacle changes,
human's need for spectacle remains nothing new?
Silly, hypothetical questions aside,
some folks, creators of the wacky and the weird,
give two and two together away
as if the sum were five.
Give us an abacus for truth.
Amen.

O that you would tear open the heavens and come down.
- Isaiah 64:1

Traveler,
who without we are wanting,
make your absence presence;
come down, show up,
blow through, be along,
for, once again,
we act alone.
Amen.

The people of long ago are not remembered.
- Ecclesiastes 1:11

Recollector,
who promised Abraham descendants
as numerous as the stars and the sand,
stuck in the middle of posterity,
descendants become ancestors,
numerous become nameless,
today becomes yesterday;
as we tread the next step
send the named ones
to surround us.
Amen.

It is an unhappy business that God has given to human beings to be busy with.
- Ecclesiastes 1:13

God Who Did All the Good Stuff Those First Six Days,
and left everything else to us,
we make joyless joy
failing to rest;
remind us:
you finished your work
at the start of the seventh day.
Amen.

"Come, let us cast lots, so that we may know on whose account this calamity has come upon us."
- Jonah 1:7

Divine Finger,
intimating and numbering and assuming
the sins of the world,
O, how we want to
know,
Who did it?
How quick we are to lay the blame
at someone else's feet
yet unwilling
- or unable -
to follow the thread
and return to the first cause.
Point us in our direction.
Amen.

It is better to go to the house of mourning than to go to
the house of feasting...
- Ecclesiastes 7:2

God of the Hovel, the Hole, the House and the Hotel,
who creates a room for each of us,
a nameplate, not a number, on the door,
which we close to keep the noise of others out
while binging-watching our own noise;
though we may shed tears for the end of a season
the well of our deep grief dries;
move us to go next door to our neighbor
who knows only tears of aloneness.
Amen.

You search out my path and my lying down.
- Psalm 139:3

Scout and Tour Guide,
who knows my ways
even before those ways
become ways of possible ways;
many feel tied down
on a one-way track to hell;
broaden our imagination
of potential pathways
so we desire life
with one another
once again.
Amen.

A voice says, "Cry out!" And I said, "What shall I cry?"
- Isaiah 40:6

Oracle of old,
Word before words,
who dances with Miriam
as horse and rider are thrown into the sea,
who plunges into the cold, closing surf
with each chariot driver,
What shall we cry?
For news is
black and white with countless grays
and the people stir by the easy way.
What shall I cry?
Make the call simple.
Amen.

Deliver me, O Lord, from evildoers!
- Psalm 140:1

Maker of weal and woe,
who confounds the paths of the innocent
while twisting the paths of the guilty,
Is it possible for the scribbled way
and the straight way to not intersect?
For when they do,
death follows.
Amen.

Go, eat your bread with enjoyment.
- Ecclesiastes 9:7a

Deliverer of bodies,
who laid out your body
on a cross and in a tomb,
who turned your body
into bread at a table,
who created the field of us;
how we all want to wave
together, swaying,
as your breath
moves across our faces;
too full to even move.
Amen.

And drink your wine with a merry heart.
- Ecclesiastes 9:7b

Grape-maker, Grape-grower,
whose vines trellis the world,
the grape-drinkers thirst
for fine vintages
that dance on the tongue
and gambol the heart.
Amen.

"...but to sit at my right hand or at my left is not mine to
grant..."
- Mark 10:40

Left-handed God,
Right-handed God,
Many-handed Gods,
we have to hand it to you;
handing to us
what is at hand
and then
we hand that power,
in hope of being chosen,
back to you.
Place faith in our hands
in our hands.
Amen.

Divide your means seven ways, or even eight, for you do
not know what disaster may happen on earth.
- Ecclesiastes 11:2

God,
who divides Creation into infinite complexity,
we have put all our eggs into the baskets of
stubbornness, selfishness, hatred,
arrogance, delusion, greed
and violence.
Weave us another basket,
a basket full of anointing oil
so we can once again cry out,
"For unto all a child is born!"
Amen.

"I have set before you life and death."
- Deuteronomy 30:11

God,
who creates chaos and destroys order,
who arranges and fells,
lean into your dream
for life a little bit more,
so the many who feel
free from your holy choice
choose life
for life's sake.
Amen.